Stone's Throw

Promises of Mere Words

Also by Gary Hotham

Books:

Breath Marks: Haiku to Read in the Dark (1999)
Spilled Milk: Haiku Destinies (2010)

Chapbooks:

Without the Mountains (1976)
The Fern's Underside (1977)
Off and On Rain (1978)
Against the Linoleum (1979)
This Space Blank (1984)
Pulling Out the Bent Nail (1988)
As Far As the Light Goes (1990)
The Wind's View (1993)
Before All the Leaves are Gone (1996)
Hair's & Hawk Circles (1996)
Bare Feet (1998)
Footprints & Fingerprints (1999)
The Sky Stays Behind (2000)
Odor of Rain (2004)
Missed Appointment: The Haiku Art (2007)
Sand Over Sand (2009)
Nothing More Happens in the 20th Century (2011)
Our Waves Meet the Ocean Waves (2013)

Stone's Throw

Promises of Mere Words

Haiku by
Gary Hotham

PINYON PUBLISHING
Montrose, Colorado

Copyright © 2016 by Gary Hotham

All rights reserved. Except as permitted under the U.S. Copyright Act of 1976, no part of this publication may be reproduced, distributed, or transmitted in any form or by any means, or stored in a database or retrieval system, without the prior written permission of the publisher, except for brief quotations in articles, books, and reviews.

Design by Susan Elliott

Photograph of Gary Hotham by Kimberly Hamrick

First Edition: June 2016

Pinyon Publishing
23847 V66 Trail, Montrose, CO 81403
www.pinyon-publishing.com

Library of Congress Control Number: 2016939335
ISBN: 978-1-936671-33-5

Thank You

To some talented co-workers and friends, now retired, who quietly watched the nation's back for many years:

Robert (Rob) K. Appleton; Grover C. Hinds III;
C. Harold Hutcheson; Kenneth (Ken) R. Madison;
Lester (Les) Myers; E. Edison (Ed) Orr;
Dale L. Roberts.

Thanks to those who have made helpful suggestions as to which haiku should go into the collection. I appreciate your thoughtfulness and your time taken to build this collection.

And thanks to Jaroslav Pelikan for his thoughts on mere words.

Preface

I like this statement by Czeslaw Milosz for what I think it says about words:

"Poetry feeds on the remembrance of our perceptions that are no more, since they belong to a moment in the past."

Words give our perceptions longevity and endurance. Words give the perception a life of its own and it is not lost in the past or something that floats around in one's memory making brief appearances from time to time. The world one sees and experiences is defined by language. A deeper or greater understanding of the world comes by testing and refining it with more words or better words. Pointing at the same scene or event to another person is not the same as explaining it with words. Without words the world is the child's dark closet of unknowns. Words are an important light for one's life.

Czeslaw Milosz, *A Book of Luminous Things: International Anthology of Poetry* (1996), p. 139.

cloudless
walls not as old
as the stones

unaffected
by the earth's curve
our row of tomato plants

in season
more butterflies
than afternoon plans

early morning walk
last year's meaning
changes

cloudy night
places starlight goes
in a lifetime

more reasons
more fireflies
than words

the foot of the mountain
the stars make us
wait

tied up fishing boats
gulls giving sunrise
        sound

far from home—
the easy words
filled in

colors missing from sunrise
parts of the snow
stay snow

up to the fisherman's knee
the world under
the ocean

extra cold

—

stars in their expected
places

folding the map
part of the country ends
in the ocean

her garden
the watering can left
in the rain

dew hanging on the fence—
paint chips off
the danger sign

after the nap—
the air pushed around
by the infant's hands

her hospital room—
snow filling the small field
next to the big one

clouds further apart—
our daughter kicks the stone
off the path

half heard rain—
page after page
of family photos

her sigh
the apple rolls off
the kitchen table

the lifeguard gone—
the sound of the ocean
reaching land

our bare feet
next to each other
next to the ocean

low tide—
the stone she picks up
smooth on all sides

with numbers
my daughter knows—
the stars counted

Christmas dinner—
the handle broken off
a tradition

a slow rain now—
the bed takes up
most of the room

afternoon's end—
the space the falling snow
takes

into the grass under the horse—
rain drips off
the general's statue

at the gull's feet—
the ocean spreads itself
thin

puddle after puddle—
the bright color
of her long raincoat

the long part of the trip—
sky becomes
more sky

in the airport lounge—
the spilled coffee left
to dry by itself

by the open window—
the part of the ocean
within hearing

cool morning ground mist—
the gate handle down
to bare metal

before it turns dark—
children start a game
they've just played

between telephone calls—
the snow drifting off
from the rest of my life

dark darker—
too many stars
too far

in what's left
of our footprints—
what's left of the wave

singing
the old forms of the verb—
Christmas day

other lights
than our own—
the Milky Way

we slide her casket out—
the small loose stones
under our feet

a fly buzzes by—
a room full of people
who know the dead man

the rattle
of leftover pills—
we empty her room

among the fireflies—
children playing past
their bedtime

back road in Maine—
a fence doesn't stop the house
from falling down

after the baptism—
the river in
different places

dry air—
the dog shaking off
the ocean

home
for Dad's funeral—
not the same quiet in the kitchen

face down—
half the pile
of sympathy cards

the wave turning back—
   the deep blue
    of the sea shell

old room odors—
nothing about my past
in the mirror

under
melting snow—
our dead end street

yard sale—
a bookmark
falls out

more stone
inside the stone—
child's play

near dark—
the grand hotel drips
long after the rain

stars before the fireworks

—

the crowd makes room
for late arrivals

autumn colors
our daughter's wedding day
circled in red

near the firefly
part of the night
missing

daylight ended hours ago—
one more page
to the investigation

hanging
on our Christmas tree—
the ornament broken years ago

lights we see the world with

—

fireflies

a new state of mind
the wind doesn't turn the corner
with us

whistling
an old tune

—

spaces between spaces between stars

morning colors
nothing so black & white
as yesterday

too strong
to stay with us
spring winds

the concert's
last trumpet note
—
our place in the universe

sudden rain
no end to the universe
as we know it

New Year's day
the party hat not made
to stay on

sealing in
the ocean air
wild roses

home
only one ocean
in her shell

cluttered voices
the whole sky the color
of the crayon

hauled into air
the ocean escapes
the lobster trap

mountain tops
distant views never making
the news

waiting out the rain

—

leaves caught in the bus stop shelter

taking the photo for them
leaving room
for the Grand Canyon

leaves scatter
where the pigeon lands
first night in a new country

yesterday's snow—
the dog's path
one way

by the pool—
her lounge chair holds
the large print novel

evening loon call—
nothing makes it
call again

the shortcut
the school children take—
a new layer of leaves matted into the old

farewell dinner—
more hot coffee poured into
what's left

careful steps
rocking the boat
rocking the top of the ocean

over the parade—
a window no one
looks out of

missed appointment—
late morning sun spreading over
the faded sofa

early in the day—
I've taken someone's
missed appointment

more windows than home

—

the child's drawing

drippings from a light rain—
the only light I have on
the only light for the moth

losing count
her world too big
for words

our pond
a frog sinks
out of sight

early morning news
the blue heron lets us watch
from a distance

the crowd thins out
stars replacing
thoughts

flurries …
snow flurries …
which card to play …

the rain pouring down—
Telemann dead for years
turned up louder

not as far to go
as the light from the stars—
night overtakes us

snowflakes
no one will miss—
melt in her hand

city center
the streetcar fills up with people
who have a destination

shadows
crossing narrow roads
fireflies light-years from the first star

Dad's funeral—
the same knot
in my tie

stone's throw
the rest of north
behind us

stars
showing up
odorless

Acknowledgments

The haiku were first published by the following journals and contests:

Acorn; Beloit Poetry Review; Blithe Spirit (England); Bogg; Books & Culture; Bottle Rockets; Frogpond; Haiku Canada; Haiku Pix Review (Taiwan); Hobo (Australia); Hummingbird; Issa's Untidy Hut; Lilliput Review; Longhouse; Mainichi Daily News (Japan); Mariposa; Modern Haiku; Muttering Thunder; Noon (Japan); Northeast; Old Crow Review; Persimmon; Pinyon Review; Presence (England); Quadrant (Australia); Raw Nervz (Canada); Roadrunner; Setouchi Matsuyama Photo Haiku Contest (Japan); Shearsman; Snapshots; Solitary Plover; South by Southeast; Still (England); The Heron's Nest; Tundra; Whirligig (Netherlands); Woodnotes.

www.ingramcontent.com/pod-product-compliance
Lightning Source LLC
Chambersburg PA
CBHW021016090426
42738CB00007B/802